WATERFALL OF LOVE

WATERFALL OF LOVE

Muriel Hoff

Written by Muriel Hoff
Edited- David Hoff and Muriel Hoff
Published by David Hoff
674 Prospect Avenue Suite 302
Hartford, CT 06105
Email: Dhoff@sbcglobal.net

Copyright 2019 by Muriel and David Hoff
First Edition 2018-100 copies
Second Edition in 2019

All rights reserved, including the rights of reproduction in whole or in part in any form.
please visit her website
www.MessagesFromMuriel.com.

Books By Muriel Hoff

Animal alphabet rhymes for children to 90

Messages via Muriel

The Voice in the Middle of the Night

Inspired Poems from the Universe

Chosen To Channel

Poetry Also Appearing In Anthologies:

More Than Magnolias

Writer's Choice

Women Of The Piedmont Triad

Edge Of Our World

A Turn In Time

The Voice Within

Wordworks

Fire And Chocolate

Soundings Of Poetry

North Carolina's 400 Years

Signs Along The Way

Here's To The Land

DEDICATION

My eternal thanks and gratitude to my late husband George for his love, support and patience from the beginning of my spiritual journey into the creative process.

My special thanks to my son David for his support and faith in my poetry and all the time spent on compiling and editing this book.

Love to my children Cindi, Steve, David and in memory of my daughter Rio (Ellen). Thanks to my daughter-in-law Nina, my granddaughter Esther, and my son-in-law Daniel and his wife Mariana.

Muriel Hoff

INTRODUCTION

The love poems included in this book Waterfall Of Love are among my favorite poems because they awaken in me, and I hope my fellow readers, a sense of tranquility, peace and a closer relationship to God and all humankind.

All my poetry was channeled from the most inspirational and challenging inner revelations of my lifetime.

I began to experience myself opening up to new levels of heightened sensitivity and perception while taking a course on the Psychology of Creativity. I began noticing peculiar sensations such as the skin of my face flushing, although my temperature was normal, squinting to read as if I had become light sensitive, and overwhelming feelings of universal love that often brought tears. I later learned that these were physical signs that were the beginning of a creative process.

I believe that channeling is an accurate term for the activity of my creative process. When this channeling process began, I would find myself awakened during the late night hours by a voice in my head reciting one or two lines of poetry. I strongly felt as if I was commanded to get out of bed and see if other lines of poetry would follow. I would take a pen and a sheet of paper or the cardboard from a new pantyhose package and then go into a dimly lit room: keeping my eyes half closed so I wouldn't be completely awakened and ready to go back to sleep.

In my first experience of this nighttime channeling, I began writing the first line I had heard when a strange thing occurred. I felt the pen start to move by itself and the words tumbled out as if I was taking dictation from an invisible source. As I finished one poem another poem would start on a different subject and others would follow until the entire sheet of paper was full. I would even write in all the margins.

The next day I typed up what I had written and though some words were scribbled, I could figure them out. The titles of the poems were always added afterwards.

I honestly feel that these inspired poems were given to me as a gift, and I also know that the reason I was chosen to receive them was to enable me to give this gift back to you, and you, and you. Enjoy.

Muriel Hoff

Greensboro, North Carolina

Where there is life there is hope.

If a tiny spark remains

it can be fanned

with love and understanding,

and it will slowly burn.

*I will give you my love freely,
I am my own person.*

*My love must flow motivated by
tenderness and appreciation.*

*Don't take me for granted
or I will harden my heart.*

*How do we attain that relationship
between parent and child
that makes the family a union,
and not a disaster?*

*There must be confidence
on both sides.
The doors must be open.
The wells and dams have to burst
and then be repaired.
There always has to be acceptance
of ideas, of distrusts, and all the
things that gnaw at the heart.
There must be empathy, and above
all a sense of humor.
For in all the doldrums there is
always a light side, and optimism
prevails when pessimism dampens
and drowns the spirit.*

*Love is an emotion
of the heart.*

*Love does not listen
to what the brain says.*

*Love is independent unto itself,
and often wears itself on the sleeve
of it owner,
vulnerable, but unafraid.*

Life is for the living.

Lets live it to the fullest.

We have inherited the earth.

Lets take on responsibility and rise to the occasion.

*The earth will respond
and give all the good things,
and we shall be as parents of a
loving child, happy and fulfilled.*

*Marriage is a two-way street.
Many contracts are torn up because
the parties didn't attempt to negotiate
a settlement.
There has to be a two-way stretch of
the mind and imagination.
Love can wreak havoc, but it can
create the most beautiful and
enduring friendship.
Love is a give and take, and usually
there is more taking than giving.
If reversed, the situation
is much improved,
for to give and expect nothing in
return is a good virtue.*

*You can create
your own destiny.*

*Have confidence in
your own abilities.*

*Give charity and do loving
acts of kindness.*

*Hope and charity
will walk the streets
together giving
love to mankind.*

*There is a deep, deep craving
within each person to be loved.
Indicative of this is the fact
that they open up to each
new adventure with hope
and a yearning for discovery.
There is deep, deep garden inside us,
a seed that develops
into a beautiful flower,
the flower of love.
It opens its petals to the sun
and craves the warmth
it sorely needs to flourish.
Love leaves you in turmoil many
times, but it is worth the excitement
because of the long range benefits.*

Is the love
that comes like a flash flood
fast and furious
the best one?

Or the love that simmers
and flounders
and falters
and finally gains momentum.

*Love between man and woman
is a bittersweet milieu of taste and
smell, clinging to –breaking up—
getting together.*

*A game played by two people with
very high stakes.*

*Sometimes a false move can destroy
your life forever, but usually it is a
learning experience,
and you who venture out to love
are the recipient of a prize.*

*Know yourself, and in knowing you
will attain a pleasant disposition.*

*Know yourself, for in knowing you
attain stature.*

*Give yourself, and in giving the
pleasantness will reward till eternity.*

*Give yourself, for in giving all the
earth is sweeter and ennobled.*

*Control yourself, for in controlling you
will become pleasant to others.*

*Control yourself, for in controlling you
hold the reins.*

Oh my princess, you awake at dawn dewy eyed.

Your arms outstretched awaiting your love.

He comes on angel's wings and his step is light.

He walks without fear, guided in the strength of your love.

His arms reach out to you, and you enter the circle unafraid and unashamed.

*Love is the challenge of the heart.
It tickles your fancy, and often makes you feel as gay as a young calf romping in the hay.
Love makes everything happy and sad at the same time.
You often see beauty where none other sees it, and tears come easily if your vanity is pricked.
If you are oversensitive, a kind word can raise you to the highest heaven, but a lover's quarrel takes you down to the subterranean depths.
You roll on merrily gathering posies for your true love, uphill and down, often collecting many bruises along the way.
The path of love is not smooth, but anything that's worth its weight is worth fighting for.
An ideal won, an ideal lost.
Measure your love carefully.
You have to live with your decisions.*

Shake the tree

of tomorrow's dreams.

You can make happiness happen.

Peel the layers laid on you.

Change your myth to reality.

Love yourself one small measure.

Say "I am and I will do" and be.

*Youth has its day,
short-lived but full
of throbbing expectations.*

*There is first love,
the heart opens and the pulse
beats with rapidity.
The heart is a drum beating away;
all the senses are caught up
and enraptured.*

*It is a pure unequivocal moment
that can never be repeated in exactly
the same way.*

*Each experience is a new tomorrow.
Many times the bloom of first love
is short-lived, the buds wither
before they have even ripened.*

Treat everything with importance.

*Respect the young and the old,
being pleasant to them, for the years
thunder ahead, and soon
you will be white and old.*

*The child you smiled at may have
smiled at another and another,
and the reward will finally be yours
when the smile is returned to you.*

Words of praise sincerely given,
enriching the spirit,
caressing the heart,
enables the recipient
to proudly smile
and say "thank you".

In return, the donor
of the praise
receives the gift of
well-being and satisfaction
for doing this
deed of loving kindness.

Look and behold around you.

*Blazing forth on the horizon,
day in – day out
are the revelations of love,
of care and of wonder.*

Tune in to the glory.

*Tune out the mediocre,
mendacity, and greed.*

*Tune in to the simple pleasures:
the love of the land,
the people who till the earth's soil;
the people who fill needs not
necessarily their own.*

*And do so with humility
and pleasure.*

If you give unconditionally

with heart and soul

the love that lies within

not expecting anything in return

not limiting or changing another

then your mind will

be engulfed

in peace.

Beauty is often

in the eye of the beholder,

but true beauty is deep inside.

True beauty has a way

of emerging and giving renewal

with a feeling of peace.

FORGIVENESS
Will set you free

FORGIVENESS
The way for you and me

FORGIVENESS
With love and without pity

FORGIVENESS
Brings peace and clarity

FORGIVENESS
The only way truly to be

FORGIVENESS
Will set you free

*How will I know my true love when
she comes along?*

*She will wear daisies in her hair,
in her eyes will be the innocence of
an angel.*

No guile will cloud her vision.

*Her purity will shine forth in a
luminescent glow.*

*Love your neighbor
even finding his actions hateful
until he, feeling the light of your love,
draws upon your inner strength.*

*Then like a sick person healing,
so shall he in the light
of your love eliminate hateful actions,
and emulate your good ones.*

*It is a dominion of the senses,
a strengthening of the powers
of concentration,
till one actually loses the
seeds of hatred and plants
the seeds of love in one's heart.*

*If I came to you
and all my branches were barren,
would you render me useless,
or would you see me
in a new type of splendor?*

*If I came to you in awe,
unashamed, and unadorned
would you let me bask
in the light of your love?*

*Giving charity
is like
a drop in the ocean
of love.*

*All the drops
ferment together
and form
a vortex of living.*

"If love awaits where will I find it,"

says the maiden

"it will find you"

*To love is to be a sponge,
soaking up the signals,
intercepting as an antenna that picks
up energy output and
tunes in on gravitational pulls.*

*To love is to be a soft shoulder,
a gentle touch,
and always a loving friend,
capable of forgiveness,
ready to console and heal wounds.*

*What are friends for,
if not to be near
when trouble beckons,
and when happiness spreads
her wings on the horizon?*

Love justice and mercy,

love your fellow man

and treat him as your brother,

never admitting the slightest twinge

of envy.

Immerse yourself in good deeds.

Like a cloak, they will protect you

from harm.

Love, love, love

makes the world go round,

causes traffic to stop,

hops, skips, jumps

over the brambles and wires

and leads to the eventualities

it finds itself addicted to.

Love goes in circles

and comes full turn,

tantamount to the earth

spinning on its axis.

Love doesn't give warnings.

She can be as tempestuous

as the winter wind on a stormy sea,

or as gentle as the summer breeze

floating across a silvery lagoon.

Love begins as a small flame

and grows and grows,

nurtured from within.

Like a seed it continues to flourish

till it bursts forth in full bloom—

a thing of great beauty.

Love is a vast binary,

a storehouse of intricate emotions

filed under repressive codes.

Its nature is analogous

to the beast that preys on

our soft side taking advantage.

It is in this condition that man

often makes unwise decisions

affecting other people.

*Woman is the essence
of all loveliness.*

*In youth she blooms like a rose
and as she slowly sheds her petals,
the odor of her perfume
lingers upon your nostrils.*

*Age enhances her beauty,
experience molds her character,
she is all things to man.*

*My love is so strong,
my commitment so firm,
my faith so true,
that walls of iron melt.*

*Fear approaches,
but draws away and disappears.*

No obstacle can keep us apart.

*No challenge is so great,
that it can't be conquered
by us together.*

In the circle of your love

I feel loved

my hurts are healed

I am never alone

I am made strong

I can achieve.

In the circle of your love

all things are possible.

Look not to others to fill your cup,

look inside yourself.

If you have love

inside yourself

you can share it

with others.

*Give love
not a token of remembrance.*

*Give love
a renewal of your covenant.*

*Give love
for yesterday, today and tomorrow.*

*Give love
with utmost faith and devotion.*

*Give love
to all creatures large and small.*

*When you give love
all the earth is ennobled.*

*Give love
a smile
a hug
an arm to lean on
a challenge for betterment
a door opening to a new tomorrow.*

*Give love
this gift worth more
than precious jewels can give hope
to the afflicted, can ease suffering,
and can warm a heart
that has been frozen.*

*Give love
you will grow in a new direction.
you will shine from the inside,
you will enrich many lives,
you will bring warmth
in the cold of winter.*

Purity of the heart

is often described

as a most worthwhile virtue.

The heart is

the recipient of love.

Love waits

and plays

the game of hide and seek.

Many hearts

are turned inside out

following topsy turvy flights

of uncertainty, and often despair.

*If I could gather my love
into a bouquet,
I would give it to you
singing praises in dulcet tones.*

*Oh my love, how honored I am
to share in this grandiose scheme.*

How rewarding your love.

*Parents give your children ideals,
for in the home lie the lessons
of the world.*

*Set good examples,
practice what you preach,
and always be there
when needed for advice.*

*Always be honest, a child knows
when a parent pretends.
Every time you falsify,
you drop a niche in their ladder,
until the ladder topples,
and in fear and confusion the
children will listen to other voices.*

*Never give up hope,
for in every child's heart
they still want their parents love.*

*They will come back,
but be ready to receive them.
Look into their hearts
for there is the only answer
to true understanding.*

Love lingers

on past performances,

throwing in your face

endless encounters,

often ignoring the

simple noble deeds

and occurrences.

Love is a flower opening,

beautiful, innocent,

untouched by human hands.

It fades –all its glory

a haunting memory.

*If you wait long enough you see
many things that make you realize
the value of patience.*

*It is easy to fly off the handle, and
then wonder why you have created
such a commotion.*

*Why do the very people you love act
stunned and hurt as if you had hit
them over the head with a hammer?
A sensitive person cannot stand the
loud vibrations of yelling.
It produces static and tears deep into
the psyche, sometimes causing
irreparable harm.*

*Learn control.
Discipline if used correctly with love
is a welcome addition to family living.*

Love

has no friends

with the likes

of deceit and treachery.

These are used for

purposes alien

to love's true nature.

Love

is like a message,

swift and true

crossing chasms

and oceans

to reach deliverance.

Love

is a two-sided affair.

If it is played as a game,

the rules should be fair

and not favor one above the other.

Love

knows many nooks and crannies

where it tries out experiments.

Some are successful

and some are not.

Love

makes the earth

move under you.

Love

is the ecstasy

of a thousand violins

playing simultaneously,

as you go from one level

of consciousness to another.

*Do not let contrite thoughts
dominate you.*

*Think not of how
you love yourself,
but how you love others.*

*Seek them out,
aid and assist them.
Cast an eye in the direction
of the unknown to you.*

*Let the milk of kindness
flow like water escaping from a
faucet left wide open.*

*Spread the joy.
Let happiness reign.
Walk hand in hand
with your brother and sister.*

In the light

of your love

anger, pain, and frustration

will disappear.

When you

find the gift of peace,

the world will be a better place.

*Within our primal core
there exists a tenderness and love
that waits to be returned.*

*Character is formed very early
but it is never too late
to mold the clay.
Learning is a fruity drink
simmering, bubbling ,and boiling.
A wisdom brew emerges.
You imbibe and become imbued
with the pulp of knowledge.
The knowledge to be metered out,
and shared from
generation to generation.*

Any day, any minute, any hour
a miracle will ensue.
A child is born
a miracle happens
a dream is answered.
An awakening of the soul and spirit,
a vision of loveliness.

This globe of humanity,
a soul within a soul
pulsing with the mystery of life,
heralding the emergence of a
new entity birthed in pain and joy.

This burden of love,
squeal of the universe
fresh born fruit
child of sweetness,
the world awaits.

Ah the sweet, sweet love,

the tender moments

that may or may not

match eternity.

My heart is a brook

that bubbles

merrily, merrily, merrily

gaining momentum

on the way.

*A truly good man will
protect the poor and rich alike.
In his soul is the true wonder.*

*Pure and beyond reproach,
from him flows the love and devotion
of many years of training.*

*No guile has he,
only the fervent desire to
group together all the miscast,
the abused, and the unloved.*

*For can it be said that life has power
without compassion,
or that life has meaning
without the strata of imagination?*

And so I come

to you

with

all my love,

all my heart,

all my strength,

a fountain filled with hope,

ever full of love.

*Look out the window of love
and see how cherished ideals
are broken and lay wasted.*

*If need be we must mend
the broken pieces.*

*Life is one big jigsaw puzzle,
and the pieces have been scattered
hither and yon,
but there is a magnetic pull
that demands to fit the pieces
together in harmony.*

*Think not of how
you love yourself,
but how you love others.
Seek them out,
aid and assist them.
Cast an eye in the direction
of the unknown to you.
Let the milk of kindness
flow like water
escaping from a
faucet left wide open.
Spread the joy.
Let happiness reign.
Walk hand in hand
with your brother and sister.*

Love

has a way of catching rainbows

and then destroying them.

Enter the pathway of love,
let it envelop you
and casual relationships
become sacred friendships
penetrating all your inner feelings
and your heart.

Love is all around you
encircling you in a great wash of
tenderness and mercy.

Enormous feelings of love penetrate
to the very soul of you.

You are blissfully happy and content
to live in this space surrounded by
the beauty of love.

*I am a river with many tributaries
joining into me.*

I give of myself to help others.

*I cool a troubled vision and soothe
an aching soul.*

*Lovers throw pennies into me
and make wishes.*

*I am something different
to each passing wanderer,
foe to some and friend to others.*

Let us
make poetry, not war.

Let us
sing songs of love, not hate.

Let us
praise, not condemn.

Let us
join together in peace.

*Your love shall light the hearts of a
nation and make it mighty.*

*Your faith shall bind the wounds,
heal the injured,
bring forth a renaissance of ideas
and a flowering of plans.*

*Fruit will drop from the
vine at your feet,
and you shall share the sweetness
and goodness with all.*

*Illumination
shall light your way,
and history
shall remember your deeds.*

*My child, blood of my blood,
flesh of my flesh
conceived in love.*

*How far a path you have traveled,
so many detours.*

*Yet there is an invisible bond,
an invisible cord that ties us together.*

*With patience, fortitude, and a kind
demeanor without blaming others,
but accepting your responsibilities,
you will achieve success
and happiness, and on the way
lose remorse and resentment.*

*To be in your presence will bring
love and happiness.*

*Whoever shows enmity,
let him not show his face,
but rather let him go forward
never to tongue words ill-used.*

*Temper your words
and train yourself
to halt enmity
and replace it
with love and trust.*

Oh mothers of the night,
your cries reach out
all over the world.
"Let love invade the boundaries
of men's hearts.
We pray for a cessation of war,
for peace and love
to reign supreme.
We pray for strength
of body and soul
to enable us to do good deeds
to repair the world."

Seek out the fineness

and purity in people.

Man is but an empty shell

when he is alone.

Man glimmers and glows as he

experiences the warmth of a smile,

the encouragement of a hearty hello,

and the genuineness of an open

heart that turns in his direction.

Find the strong bond of

friendship and love.

How does it happen that often people converse, but behind the conversation it is empty?

The spirit lacks confidence, empathy, and determination to achieve a peaceful concordance, and in its place is an emptiness of disastrous consequences. Alleviation of this inertia can be attained by a meeting of the minds, drawn together by mutual love, understanding, and striving, to achieve a union of thought and action.

There must be a division of the responsibilities, and a growing together that produces harmony. Inexperience does not matter. What counts is the desire to achieve a union of order and empathy, a closeness of thought and action, a growing together of brotherhood, an aorta of love and peace.

*What can be done
to encourage
love and brotherhood?
Show me the light,
manifest in me the love
of my brother,
that I may raise him up,
and send him my love,
so that it may envelop him,
and make him spread that love
around and around.*

*My wishes are scattered like stars
in the heavens,
wishes waiting to come true.
I wish you success in your
endeavors, lightness of spirit,
and gobs of golden light
to shine upon you.
I wish that in the bumps of life
you land gently,
push yourself up and start again.
I wish you courage and
steadfastness to pursue your
dreams, clearness of mind to
decipher your problems
and solve them.
I wish you to know love,
and for you to be helpful in society
to others less fortunate.
People need people, and you have a
sweet loving nature.
I wish you patience, fortitude
and stick-with-it-ness
to achieve your goals.
All this I wish you and many more.*

ABOUT THE AUTHOR

Muriel Hoff was born in New York in 1923 and has lived in Greensboro, North Carolina since 1954. Her poetry has appeared in numerous anthologies. She is a founding member of the Writer's Group of the Triad. She won the first Greensboro Poetry Slam sponsored by the International Poetry Review. The University of North Carolina at Greensboro archives her complete works. The University of Hartford hosts the Muriel Hoff American Jewish Poetry Award at the Maurice Greenberg Center for Judaic Studies.

Muriel is a lifetime member of Hadassah and a past President of Beth David Sisterhood in Greensboro. She has written the cover poems for the Beth David Synagogue High Holiday booklet for the past 50 years.

www.ingramcontent.com/pod-product-compliance
Lightning Source LLC
Chambersburg PA
CBHW051410290426
44108CB00015B/2223